Facebook® Party Secrets
of a
Million Dollar Party Girl

By Lynn Bardowski

Success Secrets of a Million $ Party Girl

Rave Reviews!

"Lynn's Facebook Party strategy has totally changed my business! I've doubled my sales and moved up to the #1 Director in the country. Thanks to Lynn! Within weeks of changing over to her party formula I sold over $3K and sponsored 6 recruits!"
- Joy Farley, BeautiControl

"I could seriously just hug you Lynn Bardowski! I booked a party before I had even plugged into Lynn's system fully, because I knew it would force me to sit down and go through her videos and take action! I'm really glad that I did. I sold over $850, booked 3 more parties, the guests really enjoyed the way I did the party, which only took me 35 minutes tops.
- Tiffany Bostick, Pure Romance

"I no longer have to wonder who to ask to Host my next party, thanks to the Pick a Date, Pick a Prize game and door prize slip (using Google Forms). Both have been game changers for my online parties, helping me to book more parties and identify potential recruits."
- Stacey Killam, Younique Blue Status Presenter

"I closed my first FB party (using Lynn's strategy) at $657 in sales and one booking! Woot woot! The second one closed over $400 with 3 bookings! I love posting "how do you know the host" with an original photo of the Hostess (vs. the same "roll call" graphic everyone else is using). Once guests comment about the host they seem to really open up and make more comments and participate in the posts that follow."
- Arilys Palacios-Nisler, Partylite

"HUGE Thank YOU for your Facebook Party course!!!
Still learning and improving every single day! Last Sunday I
had a goal to sell $892 by Midnight...I sold $909 on
Facebook. Did two FB LIVE parties (30 minutes each) and
then some follow up. LOVIN learning Facebook Tips,
Techniques, Marketing and more from Lynn!"
- Gwen Helmka, Signature Home Styles

**"After 20+ years in the biz Lynn walks the walk and talks
the talk.** She is so relatable that EVERYONE can benefit from
her trainings. The 1st book (Success Secrets of a Million Dollar
Party Girl) was a fun, easy read that will make you laugh out
loud."
- Robin Guillard, Jewelry Girl

"Lynn is the REAL DEAL! Her knowledge and expertise will
take your business to the next level, and she makes it easy to
implement and accomplish what YOU want to achieve! You
will learn so much from the Million Dollar Party Girl!"
- Kelly Astbury, Younique

Facebook® Party Secrets
of a
Million Dollar Party Girl

By

Lynn Bardowski

Facebook® Party Secrets of a Million Dollar Party Girl

Copyright © 2017 Lynn Bardowski

Bardowski, Lynn. Facebook® Party Secrets of a Million Dollar Party Girl
ISBN: 978-0-9990662-0-1

Published by Million $ Party Girl Press
www.milliondollarpartygirlpress.com

Printed in the United States of America
First Edition

Cover Design: Jessica Kupferman jessicakupferman.com
Editor: Betts McCalla www.runningquailpress.com
Head Shot Photographer: Dana Romano Photography
http://www.danaromanophotography.com/

Dedicated to my husband Bill, who encourages me to keep blazing new trails.

Introduction

Lynn Bardowski, awarded top 101 Women in eCommerce, is the founder of Million Dollar Party Girl—the go-to website for women in direct sales where Lynn shares her two decades plus of direct selling expertise and knowledge. As a working mom, Lynn followed her inner Visionista and had the courage, vision, and belief to leave the safety net of a successful corporate career to pursue her own personal dream of "empowering a gazillion women to discover their glow." She overcame fear, failure, and mommy guilt to become a multimillion-dollar revenue-generating entrepreneur.

According to a recent Wall Street Journal Small Business report, "Just 1.8% of women-owned businesses generate more than $1M in annual revenues." That puts Lynn at the top of her game. A keynote speaker, #1 best-selling author of *Success Secrets of a Million Dollar Party Girl,* Facebook Party strategist and blogger, Lynn is a sought after Direct Sales expert featured on Huff Post, Forbes, CBS, Fox, Enterprising Women Magazine, and more.

Lynn's philanthropy has included rolling up her sleeves to lead a team of volunteers at a local soup kitchen and supporting women's causes near and dear to her heart. As the Membership Director for the NAWBO SJ

Board 2014-2016, Lynn helped bring training and resources to women entrepreneurs in her local community.

Lynn's visionary leadership has allowed her family to live an amazing life, with many dreams come true. They've stood together on the edge of the Grand Canyon, taken an airboat through the Everglades, hiked through a rain forest, viewed Paris from the top of the Eiffel Tower, experienced Phantom of the Opera in London and New York, and drove through a volcano. A Jersey girl at heart, Lynn enjoys putting her toes in the sand and celebrating life with her husband of 33 years, Bill, and their growing family, including two grandchildren.

Contact Lynn for speaking inquiries:
www.milliondollarpartygirl.com or
lynn@milliondollarpartygirl.com

First Things First

Before you schedule your first Facebook Party – or follow any advice in this book – check with your direct sales company about their social media and online selling policies. Most companies have specific guidelines that you must follow.

Facebook® Party Secrets of a Million Dollar Party Girl

Even with decades of multimillion-dollar direct sales success, I was still struggling to find my Facebook Party groove. My online party results were mediocre at best, which was pretty frustrating. It finally dawned on me that maybe I'd been over-thinking this whole Facebook Party thing.

Going back to basics I focused on the same success strategies I created for home parties, and booked three Facebook Parties to give my new and improved Facebook Party a test run.

Three parties quickly turned into 15 Facebook Parties. Three months later I'd held 40 Facebook parties and generated over $13K in online sales. Forget partying in my PJ's. With a smartphone in hand, I could party anywhere, anytime. I even held a Facebook Party during an impromptu happy hour with my super supportive hubs. He thought it was hysterical that I could literally pay for a fun night out while enjoying a fun night out.

My How-to Facebook Party Success book explains all, including my exact easy-to-duplicate strategy, scheduling tools, and the latest and greatest in your online party toolbox...Facebook Live.

If you've read my first book or follow me on Social Media you might already be familiar with our #Visionista Community. If not, welcome to our nonjudgmental world of women helping women. Imagine that. Here's my definition to keep you in the know:

Visionista

A woman who knows who she is, where she's going, and guides her tribe of leading ladies to the top.

On to creating a fun authentic online party that builds relationships and provides a better experience – for both the Consultant and the Customer!

Step 1
How to Get Started Booking Facebook Parties

Facebook Parties, like any good marketing plan, should be one of many hosting options you are offering your customers. I'm not a fan of putting all your eggs into one party basket, and that includes limiting yourself to only holding Facebook Parties, or only holding home parties. If you want to grow, learn how to do both Facebook and home parties well. The good news is that my strategy can be easily adapted to both home and online parties. Keep it simple and duplicatable so that others can follow your future million-dollar party girl lead.

The easiest way to book more Facebook Parties with friends is to use your Facebook personal timeline to generate leads. As long as it's done in a non-salesy way.

Keep in mind that Facebook's terms and conditions clearly state that "you will not use your personal timeline primarily for your own commercial gain, and will use a Facebook Page for such purposes." In other words, only post about your business once in a while and even then, you should not include links or use ad-looking graphics.

The whole point of social selling is to connect with people, not actually sell. Otherwise, we'd refer to Facebook as "advertising media." My rule of thumb is this: If it looks like an ad and sounds like an ad, don't post it.

That means your cover photo should not promote your biz or include photos of your products. Your friends want to see an adorable picture of you and your family or furry friends, which builds the "like, know, and trust factor"—also known as the reason people buy from you.

Try something like this, but put it into your own words:

Hey friends! You probably know I'm a rep for _____. Well, I'm trying out a new online party and I need a few volunteers to test it out. Any takers?

Make your post social and not salesy by adding a personal photo. For example, hold up a Volunteers Wanted sign and shoot a selfie. Include your kids, pets, or take a car selfie for even more LIKES. In case you didn't know, car selfie pics look awesome because of the natural lighting. Take a photo standing in front of a window and you'll see what I mean. Takes 10 years off.

Increase your reach and upload your photo to Instagram first, toggling the "share on Facebook" button so it also appears on your timeline.

Here's another social way that I've used an original photo to book more parties from my personal timeline.

This post resulted in 53 LIKES, 9 Comments, and 5 parties booked that generated over $2K in sales within 3 weeks:

Every time you get a response, comment and tag the person on your original post to let them know you'll PM them. Keeping the convo going on your post is a little secret that lets Facebook know your post is engaging, which means they'll show it to more people and keep it in the News Feed.

The beauty of online parties is that very little prep is needed from the hostess. Control your calendar and offer a date within a 7-day period so you can reach your monthly goal plan and increase your income immediately. That's crazy good for your bank account.

Visionista Power Tip:

After holding Facebook parties in multiple time zones, I found the best nights to hold Facebook Parties are Monday, Tuesday, or Thursday at 9pm EST, which is friendly for most US time zones. Check in with your hostess first to see if there's anything happening on a specific night of the week that will prevent her friends from attending. For example, Wednesday nights are reserved for church service in many areas of the US, and on Friday nights in the Fall your party guests may be at the local high school football game.

Step 2
You Dated a Facebook Party! Now what?

Congratulations! You took action on the ideas in Step 1 and dated a Facebook Party or two. Yay you! Now what?

Make Sure You Are Friends With Your Hostess:
You're probably already Facebook Friends with the person who booked the party, but hey, a friend might have shared your super cute selfie with her friends. If your new hostess is not on your friends' list, send a friend request.

Say Thank You and Confirm the Date:
Just like a home party, send a "thank you for dating a party" message or note to confirm the date and time. Facebook Messenger is my go-to for immediate follow-up. Include a graphic, emoji, or GIF file that shows off your personality.

Here's what my thank you message looks like. The keyword to communicate here is *team:*

"Hey Alyssa, I'm so excited to team up with you to rock your Facebook party! I'll create an invite for you so you can personally text an invite to your friends before we create the event. What's your most favorite product?"

One of the biggest benefits of using Facebook Messenger is you can see that your hostess read your message. I really LIKE that. Wait for a response and reply back with your first hostess coaching tip: She'll want to limit the party invites to friends that she knows well enough to invite into her home. That's how

you get more engagement on your posts and avoid looking like a spammer.
Helps you stay out of Facebook Jail, too.

Let your hostess know you'll be sending her a save the date graphic that she can easily text to personally invite friends.

But wait—you might be wondering, why the heck don't I send the Save the Date with the Thank You message? My Facebook Party Secrets are all about strategy, and part of that strategy is building stronger relationships with your hostesses.

Relationship building begins with two-way conversations, which is how people communicate in real life.

On Facebook, it should look like this:
Send a message
Wait for a reply
Respond back to the reply
Send your next message
And so on.

On a side note: If your hostess does not reply to your first message, that's a sure sign your party might not be holding. Double-book that date to stay on track with your monthly goal. Of the 40 Facebook Parties that I booked to test my strategy, 10 canceled—meaning not even the hostess showed up—or generated zero sales. Assume that one in four parties won't hold, just like home parties.

Visionista Power Tip:

Use the Bitmoji app to create your own avatar for fun and engaging graphics to communicate with your Hostess and party guests. Search GIPHY for high-five or excited GIFs to show guests just how fun you really are. My favorite is Will Ferrell jumping up and down in one of the best scenes in Elf (the movie). Because Santa is coming! And I know him!

Step 3
Save the Date

As with home parties (you're probably noticing I'm saying that a lot), personal invites are key to increasing attendance. That holds true even more for Facebook Parties because of the overload of Facebook event notifications. The newest Facebook update separates notifications into New and Earlier. As a result, many events are getting ignored, which is why I don't even create an event until the hostess has texted Save the Date invites and has actual RSVPs.

Texting is my preferred method to get the word out because your hostess will typically get an immediate response, which builds her confidence that people will actually show up to her online party. Friends could be in the middle of an important biz meeting or out to dinner with their family but they'll instantly respond to a text message. Like it's a 911 call.

Give your hostess easy-to-copy/paste verbiage and a graphic that includes three (recommended) details:

- Date, Time + Time Zone of the Party
- First 10 to Join Prize Drawing
- What's in It for Your Party Guests: Include the total value of any specials and a whole lot of fun. For example: Over $30 in Savings! or Free Gift With Purchase!

Coach your hostess to text a party invite with this example message:
Hey (name), How are you? I'm hosting a (your company) online party and thought of you because you love (product or benefit). My consultant is doing a prize drawing for the first 10+ that join. Woot! How does that sound?

Notice I ended with an open-ended question there.

Red Stamp is a free app for creating digital invites, available on IOS and Android. Check out the Collections section to see if your direct sales company has branded graphics available for you. If not, no biggie. You can easily upload a graphic and edit font and design colors on one of the many generic designs.

Visionista Power Tip:

Use Red Stamp to create a Save the Date on the spot when you're at home parties too. By the time you leave the party, your future hostess will already have a few yeses!

Step 4
Create an Event That People Want to Join

Did you know there's just as much strategy behind creating the event, as there is to the actual party posts? Start by stepping into the shoes of your guests and ask yourself this question:

Why do I care?

As in…what is it about your Facebook party that will help an invited guest see through all the noise of yet another Facebook Party—so much so, they'll actually click on the invite to see what's going on. And maybe even respond "going."

Side Note: If you added your virtual party guest to a group without their permission, they're leaving your party faster than you can say spam alert.

Work with me on this. Close your eyes, and think of your event page as the window of your favorite store. Can you see the adorable purple dress, the chic sandals, the super fab leather tote, the dangly earrings, and the fun chunky necklace?

You're in love. You know this because you can feel the adrenaline rush taking you to your happy place. Did you just chug down a 5-hour energy chaser? Nope. That feeling is called retail therapy.

Truth is, you'd never in a million years put all that stuff together. But when you see a look you love on a store mannequin, it might make you so giddy that you just have to have it.

Why? Because the store made it easy for you to say, "I'll take that!"

Your Facebook Party event page is window dressing for your party, drawing passersby into your store. Your party posts are the mannequins and store displays creating a cohesive look so at the end of the party your customer can say, "I'll take that!"

Same thing, but without actual mannequins.

The end goal of your Facebook Party event page is to look like the window of Macy's on 34th Street in NYC at Christmas time.

And oh, there's Christmas carolers out front singing *Jingle Bells*.

And you're giving out hot chocolate with whipped cream on top. Or maybe free champagne.

Anyway, you have to work some magic to get your guests to walk into your online store and buy.

Here's how to dress your store window, as in create your event page:

Cover Photo:
You know the saying… a picture is worth a thousand words. In this case, it might be worth a thousand dollars in sales.

Use picmonkey.com or canva.com to create an engaging graphic that evokes emotion or a feeling.

Your invitee does not care about your logos, website links, or a collage of all your products. They care about how your product will actually make them feel. Or the problem you'll solve.

Ask yourself the questions your customers are asking.
For example:

• Will my home look beautiful? Show me a picture of that.

- Will I feel happy and relaxed in my super comfy LLR leggings? That's what I want to see.

- Will my skin look radiant and 10 years younger? Sign me up for that. Seriously.

Title:
Odds are, you lost your invited guests at your Facebook Party title, which might have looked something like this:

Cindy's (company name) Facebook Party!!!

You're thinking this Facebook Party is so darn exciting you need three exclamation points. Your customer is thinking spam alert. Or

Jennifer's (company name) Mystery Hostess Party!

Good call on the one exclamation point. But still…

Why do I care?
I don't.

Why? Because I get invited to 50 events (ok, I'm exaggerating) a day. And 49 of them are Facebook Parties. Or at least it feels that way to your invited guests.

Let's face it, those event titles are not screaming, "don't miss this" or even peaking the interest of an invited guest to want to click on the notification to see whatcha got.

And, what if I'm new to this whole direct sales party thing and have no idea what a mystery hostess party is? Your potential customer doesn't have time to solve your mystery.

If your Facebook Party title sounds like every other Facebook Party, that's your first clue that it's time to break free and do your own thang. That means avoiding industry jargon and getting right to the "Why do I care?" point.

Examples:
Refresh Your Home w/ (company name)
– Hosted by Cindy

Must Have Summer Jewelry from (company name) – Hosted by Amber
Stunning Holiday Makeup w/ (company name) – Hosted by Jen
Gorgeous Radiant Skin w/ (company name) – Hosted by Lyndse
(Company name) Spring Wardrobe Essentials – Hosted by Sara
Healthy Home Makeover w/ (company name) – Hosted by Denise

Side note: If you make it over, they will come.

Need some help with a creative Facebook Party title? Read BuzzFeed.com for inspiration. The writers at Buzz Feed are social savvy geniuses, creating juicy titles that are frequently clicked on and shared. If you're a busy Mom with no time for googling (or reading Buzz Feed) score a Facebook Party win the next time you're stuck in line at the local market. How, you might be wondering? Your best Facebook Party ever might be inspired by the magazine section you've been staring at for ten minutes. Take a second look at Real Simple, Glamour, Martha Stewart, InStyle and Cooking Light – or whatever magazine title is a fit for your biz.

Facebook suggests that you keep your event title short because most people are going to see it on mobile, which limits the number of words they'll see. This is uber important. Put the "why do I care" stuff in the first few words. If your hostess sent out the Save the Dates we talked about in Step 3, the virtual guests will already know it's a Facebook Party and who the hostess is.

Details:
The about section is one of the most underused elements of your Facebook Party. Done well, this section should be full of value and make it easy for your customer to shop. If you're creating your event from your business page (which makes your party searchable and shareable), you will have an About section and a Discussion section. Remind guests to click on discussion to see the party posts. Add keywords that will help your Customer find you. Try it for yourself.

Start typing a series of words in google search and you'll notice that google will share the most common searches right below the search bar. Those words are keywords.

Let's break down your detail section, line by line:
First line: Speak in your own voice and welcome guests to the party. Make it easy for party guests to shop (and avoid Facebook party guest frustration) by putting your website link toward the top. It should say something like: Hey, I'm Lynn! Kathy and I are so excited you're here! If you're ready to shop now, here's how you shop Kathy's party (ordering instructions).
Include a link to your google form, website, Facebook Group or Mobile number.

Lines 2+: Highlight your special offers by adding emojis to the front of each offer. My favorite emojis to make your specials stand out are the green check mark and colored hearts.

Last few lines: Share a little about your company, party how-to's, say thanks, and include your name and your hostess' name.

Visionista Power Tip:

After you create your event, take a look to see how it appears on mobile so you can make any edits before your hostess starts inviting friends.

Step 5
Your Virtual Introduction

At the beginning of this book, I mentioned that I do my Facebook Parties just like a home party. That includes the introduction, which is your one chance to make a great first impression.

Party guests will buy—and book a party or join your team—from you for three reasons:
They like you.
They know you.
They trust you.

Facebook Live catapults the like, know, and trust factor at warp speed. Beam your introduction into your customer's smart phone and have a two-way conversation—

just like you do in real life. A live broadcast will get more exposure and help you work around the limits of notifications.

Say hello and ask guests to share where they are from. When guests start commenting, continue to have a two-way conversation by mentioning them by name, and ask if they're new to your company or product. The introduction video will stay on your event page (unless you delete it) forever. LIKE comments and reply to replay viewers that tune in after you go live with a question that helps you learn more about their needs (as they relate to your products). When you're done, click on the upside-down arrow in the right corner to pin your live introduction (pinned posts stay at the top of the event) so you can welcome late-comers as they arrive. Guests will continue to see your smiling face and most-likely feel that they really do like you, and want to buy from you.

For example, if you sell skincare, ask: What's your #1 skincare concern? If you sell candles or melts, ask: What's your favorite scent? If

LYNN BARDOWSKI

you sell LLR, ask: What Unicorn are you looking for?

Use Emojis, Bitmoji (there's an app for that) and Stickers to add a fun factor. And is it just me, or does everyone love animated minion stickers and GIFs?

Introduction Post Objectives:

1. Share your value proposition: What is the main benefit guests will get when they attend your party? If you need help with this, ask your upline Leader.
2. Offer a free sample: Include a call-to-action to text you to get a free sample so you can get the convo off of Facebook. If you don't have affordable product samples, substitute product with a how-to video or downloadable pdf. For example, a Pampered Chef rep could send a pdf of Five Easy Recipes. Ask guests to text you the words: "(Hostess name) Party" to get their sample. This step achieves two goals:

42

- Builds the like, know, and trust factor by taking your party convo off of Facebook so you can have a one-on-one conversation with each guest to find out what they're interested in. For example: Respond to the text with a question like, Hi! What's your favorite type of candle fragrance? Or, what's your skin type? Show your personality and make a deeper connection.

- Creates a time-saving follow-up-system: Simply type in the words "(Hostess name) Party" in the message search to pull up a thread of all the guests' text messages. Reach out before the party closes to look for more opportunities to serve your customers, which will lead to increased sales, parties, and sponsoring leads. Ask open-ended questions, including: What did you like most about the (sample) I sent you? Anything left on your Wish List? Do you prefer I send you a catalog, party hosting info, or biz start-up deets?

Type your Hostess Name in the text message search box ➡

" *Relationship selling, and control of your party, starts with taking the conversation off of Facebook.*"
- Lynn Bardowski

3. Find new customers: If you created the event from your business page, the party will be both shareable and searchable. Sweet. Instead of the usual "Invite your friends!" post, encourage guests to share the event with friends that might also be interested in _____. Fill in the blank with your value proposition: a cozy welcoming

home, healthy happy living, easy holiday recipes, younger looking skin, etc. Sharing helps you expand your reach and connect with your ideal client.

And, if live-streaming is waaayy out of your comfort zone, you can do all the above with a selfie pic that tells party guests a little about yourself. You do you.

Visionista Power Tip:

Practice going live on Facebook privately by creating a secret group with a close friend or team member as your one group member. Only you and your one group member will see your Facebook Live posts. This will help you get familiar with going live and build your confidence. You can even use your secret group to practice your entire Facebook Party. Turn your camera to shoot in landscape for a wider video versus the narrow smaller portrait view.

Step 6
Build Attendance & Orders

In Step 5, you learned how a little change to your introduction—sending samples and asking guests to invite friends that would actually be interested in what you have to offer—can help you connect to your ideal customer.

Let's do more of that in Step 6. Just like a home party, do not rely on your Facebook Party event to do all the work for you. Sales and new parties will come from party guests, outside orders, and your hostess reaching out to ask friends and family to book a party. Hostess coach your hostess to keep your catalog (if available) in her purse so she can get outside orders while she's out and about. This can include orders from her coworkers, hairdresser, manicurist, bank teller, and anyone else she runs into. Also, ask your hostess, are you going to any family parties or will you see friends before the party? If yes, that's more people she can show the catalog to. Most of the time your hostess won't think of passing around your catalog to the Soccer Moms during the game, unless you suggest it. That's why it's called *Hostess Coaching.*

Follow up with virtual party guests that ordered outside of the Facebook Party to say thanks, and look for opportunities to provide the best service (and upsell)... as in help them get everything they need. There's nothing worse than a customer getting their new electric scent warmer with no melts to put in it. Not only will your customer not come back to shop, they'll most likely be getting those melts elsewhere. My guess is Target.

The other tool you can use to increase attendance is a fun prize drawing for the invited guests that said yes to joining the party.

Here's some ideas:

- First 10 to join prize drawing! Announce how many you need to join to do the first prize drawing. Example: "Share this event with your friends that love—or need—(your value proposition)! Only need two more to join to giveaway the first prize!

- Every 10 guests prize drawing! Do a prize drawing for every 10 guests that join the party.

- Party Crasher Drawing or Prize: Include a call-to-action post to "Invite a friend (hostess name) doesn't know, and welcome her in the comments so I can enter you in the drawing!

Visionista Power Tip:

Facebook Parties that are created from a business page are public and shareable. In fact, each party post is shareable so your guests can share both your event, your introduction, and your entire live party. And if you've turned on messaging (settings), you can message virtual guests directly from a comment, which is awesome for your follow-up. That means you will not lose a sale hoping a potential customer sees your message in their "others" folder because they're friends with the hostess, but not you.

Step 7
Pre-Party Engagement Posts

Pre-party posts should have one end goal in mind... to connect with potential customers and discover what their needs are so you can customize the live party to meet those needs. That's how you generate sales, parties, and sponsoring leads. If you're holding home parties, that's exactly what you're already doing when guests arrive. Duplicate that experience at your Facebook Party by greeting your guests and listening in to what their concerns and interests are.

Pre-Party engagement posts' tips:

- Post once a day (in your own voice) and ask a question that relates to your product. Use

"This or That" photos or A B, C, or D collage-type photos to make it easy for party guests to share what they love. Create your own graphics so you do not have to worry about landing in Facebook Jail for sharing duplicate content, or sharing content that you do not own the copyright for. Example:

- Timing is everything: During the weekday, schedule pre-party posts for the afternoon between 2–4pm or evening around 8pm, and consider your guests' time zone. On weekends, 10am–Noon is best.

- Reply to comments with a question so you can build rapport and learn even more about your guests.

- Offer helpful suggestions and advice before you start sharing shopping links. Sharing builds trust.

- Share value: If you have a special offer, include that in your pre-party post to give guests more reason to attend your live party and share your event. Avoid company graphics that look like an ad, and verbiage that sounds salesy. Remember, if your photo looks and sounds like an ad, don't post it.

- Use custom albums to post multiple photos in one post (CinchShare has this feature) vs. rapid-fire posting of image after image. Multiple posts in a short period of time can have two negative results: 1) Send your party guests running out the virtual door and 2) Flag you as a spammer which can land you in Facebook Jail. Less is always more.

- Increase engagement and add a fun-factor by using a word scramble in your pre-party posts. How? Create a phrase that connects with your value proposition and scramble up the letters in each word. Add the letters to the end of each pre-party post, with a call-to-action to guess the phrase by the time you go live. For example, LLR's value proposition is "Where Value Meets Comfort." When the guests figure it out they'll be repeating your value proposition over and over again.

Visionista Power Tip:

Have you added a Shop section to your biz page yet? It's pretty awesome! You can turn your Facebook Page into a shop and tag products in photos & videos (from a computer). Which means when you share the link to your album or video on a Facebook Party the shop section will appear right underneath, taking your party guest to checkout. *As with all ideas in this book make sure a Facebook shop is allowed by your Direct Sales company. In this example my shop is linking to my Amazon author page where fans can purchase my book.

This is how your video or album looks on a Facebook Party when you tag products in your shop

Step 8
The Party

Woo Hoo! It's party time! By now you should have connected with your guests and have a sense of what they are interested in. Customize your party, and show your guests you were listening by giving them exactly what they want.

My best advice? Ditch all the posts and scrolling overwhelm (I won't even mention refresh confusion) and go live, doing the actual party in one Facebook Live broadcast. Why? Because some really cool things happen when you go live:

1. Facebook auto-plays your live video (in silent mode) as a thumbnail in the notifications tab creating the perfect work around to the notifications your party guests might be missing.
2. Party guests can participate and ask questions in the comments. Keep in mind there will be a delay, so don't panic if you don't get feedback right away.
3. You can demo product live and in person! Want to share a how-to tip? Do it. Go live and show guests how to use your product, which creates the desire for guests to buy your products.
4. Your live broadcast is available to watch anytime. Guests that missed the live party can easily go back and watch the replay, which is a much better experience than scrolling through party posts to play catch up. Save your live video to your camera roll and upload it to YouTube so your hostess can share it with any non-Facebook friends.
5. If you created your Facebook party on your biz page, your live broadcast is shareable. What?! Oh yeah. Your

hostesses (and guests) can easily share the party on their personal page to increase your reach. That means someone can become a customer that was never invited to or attended the Facebook party. You might want to read that one again. I'll wait.

30 Minute Facebook Live Party Outline

Reminder Post: Coach your hostess to post a reminder during the afternoon, encouraging everyone to tune in. Her friends will pay attention to something she's posted, versus a reminder from you. Check the event page and reach out to your hostess to let her know the names of friends who RSVP'd "going" or "interested" so she can easily send a day-of-party personal text or Facebook Message reminder. Get creative to work around the limits of the notifications tab. And remember all those text messages you received in Step 5? That step just gave you control of your party follow-up. If your Hostess is not comfortable with sending "day of party" reminders (meaning she might feel pushy) you can do them yourself. Boom!

Roll Call Post: 15 Minutes Before Party Time: Grab a photo of the hostess from one of her "top 5" pictures on her Facebook profile, and post in your own voice to let your personality shine through. Say something like:
Eek! I'm going live in 15 minutes! Comment if you'll be watching the live party, and share how you know (tag hostess). She's _____!
Fill in the blank with a personal compliment: an awesome mom, funny, gorgeous, da bomb dot com, etc.

Close friends and family (her BFFs) are all potential booking leads because they might book a party to help their friend out. Take note of who shares the most 'hostess love."

Party Time: Go Live!
Start talking right away.
This might seem weird because you'll have a little delay before everyone shows up, so the first minute or two you might feel like you're

talking to yourself. That's ok, no one knows that. Your replay viewers might not stick around if the first two minutes are filled with you saying, "Is anyone here yet?" or "I'm just waiting for someone to show up before I start."

Ask a question.
Ask "Where are you from?" or "What's on your Wish List?"
With Facebook Live you can have a two-way conversation with your party guests, just like you do in real life.

Tell 'em what you're going to tell 'em.
Build your product selection around a how-to tip, and let party guests know what they will learn. You are not just selling. You are solving problems and sharing value. Deliver on the promise in your event title.

Here are a few examples that might apply to your products:
Home Decor: Five ways to makeover your front porch

Jewelry: Three ways to go from drab to dazzle
Cooking: Must have kitchen tools for busy Moms
Organizing: Five ways to clear the clutter
Skincare: Feel and look good skin care tips
Cleaning: Healthy home tips and tricks
Clothing: Eight ways to wear a dress (or skirt)

Tell 'em:
Share your awesome tips and show your products just like they do on infomercials. That's right... you now have your own infomercial. If you want some inspiration, watch a home shopping channel. As you're sharing your great tips and products, plant your booking and sponsoring seeds and engage with guests that are commenting and asking questions.

At least one (or maybe all) of the products should equal the amount an average hostess earns when they have a party. Instead of talking about the cost, share how they can get your MacDaddy must-have product by inviting friends to party.

See where I'm going here?

The guests need all the products you shared to get the whole look or end result, but maybe they can't afford it all.
Good news is...you have a solution. Host a party and get everything you showed free or at a reduced cost. Of course, you'll adapt that to fit your hostess program.

Hello more parties!

Include two Calls-to-Action:

You planted a few seeds and created the desire for guests to buy all the product you shared. Yes! You are on the way to Facebook Party boss.

Before you end your broadcast, include two key CTAs:
1. Pick a Date, Pick A Prize: Have a few gift bags on hand with dates on them, and share

that you have a few "hot" dates available! The first guests who comment to pick one of your dates, get the prize in the bag. This strategy is commonly referred to as FOMO. Fear of Missing Out. If you've been coaching your hostess for pre-bookings, you might have a party date already arranged to get the momentum going. Keep the prizes low-cost, simple, and easy to mail so your team can easily duplicate your efforts. My favorite prizes are those that can only be redeemed when your future hostess has her party on her original party date.

Prize examples:
Free hostess shipping
Extra 1/2 price item
Extra hostess credit
Free bonus gift w/ qualifying party

2. Ask me a question about my job:
After you shared your Pick a Date, Pick a Prize CTA, announce that you're giving bonus points for anyone who wants to learn a little more about your biz!

Say, "For the next minute you can ask me any question about my job and get bonus points in the door prize drawing. Go!"

If there's a time delay—or no one asks a question right away—keep talking and ask yourself a question.
Start with something like:

"The most popular question is.... "How much does it cost to get started?"

This is the question that's on everyone's mind as they watch you and see how easy it is to sell online. Share your start-up information first.

No matter what the question is, always respond with the word YOU first.

Examples:
How much does it cost to get started?
You can start for as little as $99. I started with _____.

How many parties do you do?

You can do as many parties as you choose. I do _____ parties a month to earn _____.

Do you have trips?
You can qualify for free trips every year! I've traveled to _____ or I'm working toward a trip to _____.

Do you have to attend training?
Only if you want to make money (I love to throw that in there). You can get support in our group, learn online, and at live events (if applicable).

Close:
Time for your party wrap-up!
Share that you'll be adding shopping details to your post (go back and edit to add shopping details) and point above your head to communicate where they can easily find ordering information.

You'll also want to let party guests know to come back in a few minutes for your Door Prize Drawing—also known as your lead funnel.

Use a scheduling tool to schedule your door prize slip to post a few minutes after your 30-minute live-party. Comment and tag everyone that enters to let them know you received their response and that you'll pick the winner tomorrow. That gives ample time for late-comers to participate in the party and prize drawing—which can generate more sales and leads.

Do your party Live!
*Go back and edit your post to include product details. Make it easy to shop & buy.

Party time! Come see all the summer must-haves! 🏖️☀️🌴
I have gift ideas for you too! 💜🎁🎈
Here's all the items I featured tonight:
Most awesome product evah ____
Amazing must-have ____... See More

Visionista Power Tip:

Use Google Forms to create a virtual door prize slip with a built-in follow-up system. All the answers are automatically organized for you in a spread sheet that you can access online or via the google sheets app right on your phone. If you need help with Google Forms join our community over at milliondollarpartygirl.com by clicking on the OhYeah! button. I'll send you an article with a Google Forms how-to.

Step 9
Post-Party Follow Up

The party might be over, but your follow-up is not. Remember the samples you gave out in your introduction? Type your hostess name in the text message search box to pull up a list of everyone that took you up on your offer. Reach out via personal text to find out what's on their Wish List, and offer to help with their order. You'll also want to follow up with anyone that ordered to look for upsell and booking opportunities. Take a look at each order to make sure your customers got everything they need to use your product, then personally call to say thanks, suggest add-ons, and find out what other products are on their Wish List. Personal contact builds relationships and gives you the perfect opportunity to provide more solutions, as in helping your Customer get whatever they didn't buy – but really wanted to. A party should solve that one. Say, I'd love to help you get (product) for free! How does a Facebook (or home) party sound?

Never say, Do you want to book a party? Close-ended questions almost always lead to "No" responses. Instead say,
You: Did you get everything on your Wish List?
Guest: Well...I really wanted that super fab doodad but I can't afford it right now. Boo.
You: I'd love to help you get the super fab doodad for free (or discount) by hosting a fun party. (Original Hostess name) got that *and* the bonus thingamabob! How does that sound?

Here's what to post after the party to boost sales, bookings, and get referrals.

Thank You Posts: Ongoing

Use an original graphic to share a heartfelt and timely thank-you to everyone that orders. I use the (free) Bitmoji app—which has a few thank-you avatars to choose from, so you can mix up your posts. Tag your customer in the comments (or ask the hostess to tag). This post serves two purposes: (1) You'll remind everyone who didn't shop to get on it and (2) You'll show off your awesome customer service.

And it's good manners.

Reminder to Shop Post: Next day
Schedule a "reminder to shop" post for the next day that includes three things: (1) how to shop (2) when to shop (include the date the party is closing) and (3) how to enter your door prize drawing. Your door prize is your lead funnel, so you want to make sure everyone knows they can enter—whether they shopped or not.

Door Prize Drawing Post: 1 or 2 days after the party
You might want to post "last chance to enter" before you pick your Door Prize winner. Go

live, upload a short video of you picking the winner, or take a picture of the prize with the winner's name on a piece of paper.

Breaking News Post: Party closing day
If the party had great engagement but your party sales are lagging, go live and announce breaking news on the day the party is closing. Your news could be a fun how-to or tip to encourage sales, a recap of a sale or special offer, or a shout out announcing what's on your Hostess' Wish List—and what she needs to get there. You'll also want to coach your hostess to post a final reminder to shop and share why she hosted the party.

Products Have Shipped Post: Day products ship
Don't just party and run. Highlight your great customer service by going back to the event to post that the orders are on the way. Let customers know how the products are shipping (for example, UPS or USPS) and when they can expect their order to arrive. The Bitmoji app has several graphics that

work well for this post, including your cute avatar popping out of a box.

Leave a Review Post: A few days after products arrive
If you created the event from your biz page, click on Events to see all your parties listed by date for an easy follow-up system. Go back a few days after the order arrived (and you made sure all orders were delivered okay) to ask for a review on your page, and include the link to your review page.

Reviews are an easy way to let your customers tell their friends about you and gain referrals. Reviews can also make your page stand out from other direct sellers in your company and make your page easier to find in Facebook search. To enable reviews, go to settings > reviews > allow visitors to review this page > save. Simply add the word "reviews" to the end of your page URL to share your review link in a Facebook group, email or anywhere else. Your reviews will be sorted by 3 clickable tabs at the top: Most Helpful, Most Recent and Star Rating. When you get a review show your appreciation by liking the post and saying thanks!

Visionista Power Tip:

Door prizes should be duplicatable for your team, which means you'll want to use prizes that are both affordable and easy to mail. And they don't always have to be your products. The Dollar Store is a great resource for affordable door prizes (and team recognition gifts), including cosmetic bags, jewelry holders and manicure sets. Check with your company policies to make sure any special offers or prizes are in compliance with corporate guidelines.

Step 10
Leads, Leads, and More Leads

Never party without your lead funnel—also known as a virtual door prize slip. I use Google Forms for two reasons: (1) It's free and (2) your answers are magically entered into a done-for-you follow-up system via a spread sheet.

Google Forms also has really cool features that include notifications, required questions, photo and video adds, and animated banners. Want a fun party theme with balloons blowing in the wind? They've got it.

The secret to getting more leads is to ask a limited number of open-ended, multiple-choice questions that focus on your key goals. That might include adding contacts to your email list or Facebook group, booking parties, and recruiting new team members.

For example:
Closed-ended question:
Do you want to book a party? (Um, no.)

Open-ended question:
What type of party interests you most?
Offer multiple choice answers that include Facebook Party, home party, catalog party, dual-hostess party, theme party, pop-up party, and whatever other type of party you want to book.

Open-ended questions are so powerful that out of 170+ door prize entries 61.8% responded yes to hosting some type of party. For some reason, clicking a button is a lot easier than actually saying yes. Even though they are saying yes. It's a psychological thing.

How do you follow up? Simple. Believe them. Believe when they check the Facebook Party or Home Party box (or any other box) that they really want to have a party.

You don't have to worry about being pushy because you are giving them exactly what they asked for. In fact, if you don't follow up and ask them when they want to have their party you'll lose credibility—and a hostess.

Let's say they checked the box for Facebook Party. Text messages tend to get the fastest response, so fire off a quick text with a message like this,

Hi Lauren. Thanks for entering my door prize. I'm so excited to party with you! How's Tuesday (next available date) for your Facebook Party?

Warning: Only fools rush in. Wait for a response before you start texting back about how awesome your hostess program is. You don't want to be perceived as the crazy direct sales stalker. Same goes with your Facebook

Group. Only add people that respond yes to joining your group.

You'll find more leads when you follow up after the sale. Customer service calls go a long way to turning your customers into raving fans that send referrals your way. If you don't have a referral program, create one. Tell your customers you will stock them up with (fill in the blank) whenever they send a new hostess your way (when the party holds) and recognize referrals in your customer group to get the momentum going. Other referral gift suggestions are gift certificates or a discount off their next order.

Visionista Power Tip:

Get the Google Forms notifications "add on" so you get notified via email when someone fills out your form. That will create a built-in follow up system for you. You'll find it by clicking on the puzzle piece in the "More" icon, which is represented by three dots in the right corner.

Special invitation for Book Readers!

If you're still using last year's (or last
month's) party script & need fresh ideas
watch my free webinar:

Facebook Party Success:
What's In & What's Out

Go to
http://events.milliondollarpartygirl.com/facebook to
learn how to create an authentic online party
experience that encourages guests to buy,
book and do what you do!

You got this! ~ Lynn

Apps & Websites

Scheduling & Systems

CinchShare.com	Social media scheduling and Facebook Party planning
Grytics.com	Facebook Groups scheduling, engagement tools, statistics and metrics
google.com/Forms	Create a (free) virtual Door Prize Slip
Trello	Organize your projects into boards
Google Sheets	View Google Forms responses on your phone

Photo Editing & Content Creation

PicMonkey	Online image editor
Word Swag	Make inspirational images with quotes
Canva	Create designs for all your social platforms
Photofy	Photo editing app
Bitmoji	Your own personal emoji

Video Apps & Editing

Giphy	Search and share animated GIFs
Giffer	Animated GIF-maker
Ripl	Create animated posts

Hyperlapse	Speed up videos
Boomerang	Capture your products in action
Videoshop	Add text, music & effects
Youtube Editor	Free tool to edit YouTube videos (go to Creator Studio >Create >Video Editor)

Content Curation

Flipboard	Gather & share content from social networks
Buzzfeed	Videos, quizzes, and trending topics
PopSugar	Fashion, food, beauty & health tips

Virtual Invites

| Red Stamp | Digital and paper greeting card app |

Live-Streaming & Video

BeLive.TV	Broadcasting studio for Facebook Live
Switcher Go	Add photos or video while live-streaming
OBS Studio	Free software for live-streaming
ClipGrab	Free YouTube downloader

Browser

Chrome

Fast, free, and better for Facebook Parties

63889817R00046

Made in the USA
Middletown, DE
07 February 2018